Busy Wheels

First published in Picture Lions 1973
by William Collins Sons and Co Ltd
14 St James's Place, London SW1
© Random House 1973
Printed in Great Britain
by William Collins Sons and Co Ltd, Glasgow

PETER LIPPMAN

Busy

Wheels

COLLINS
PICTURE LIONS

In the city wheels are turning everywhere.
Early in the morning dust-carts roll down
the street. Cans clatter. Men shout.

Lorries with brushes on wheels sweep the
streets and suck up the dirt.

People ride to work in buses, while mothers wheel their
babies in prams and pushchairs
Everyone is on the move!
Busy wheels help them move faster.

Some people like to move faster yet! Their racing cars zoom round and round the track while people cheer. Who will be the lucky winner?

Sometimes wheels go too fast and there's an accident. Breakdown lorries haul away the wrecked cars. Ambulances take people who have been hurt to the hospital.

When a fire breaks out, the fire-engines come as fast as they can. Whistles blow. Sirens wail. Cars get out of the way.

Fire-engine wheels are very important.

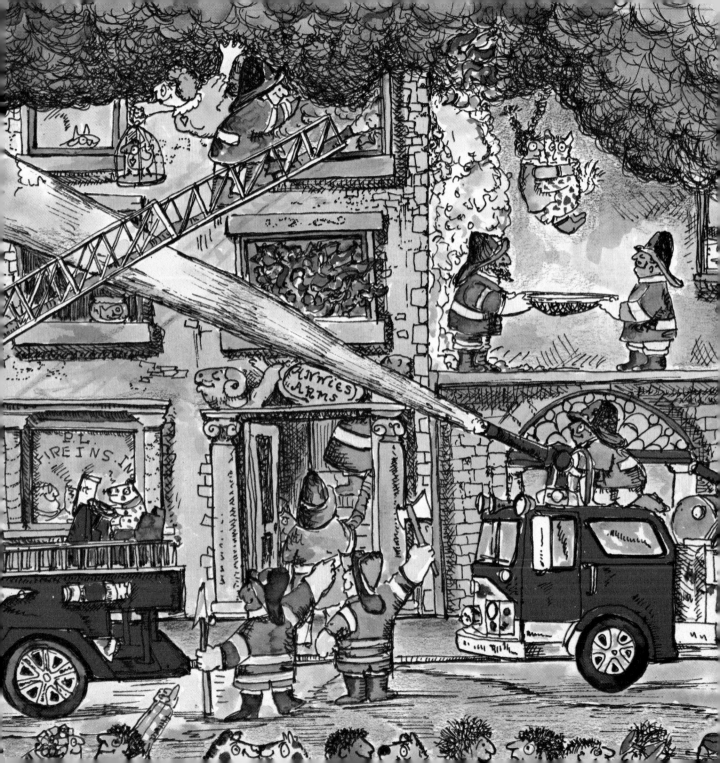

Busy wheels help to build roads, too. Bulldozers and diesel shovels dig up the dirt. Dumper trucks move it out of the way. Big heavy steam-rollers go back and forth, flattening the roadbed.

In the country other kinds of wheels are at work. Tractors pull the farmers' ploughs and wagons. Combine-harvesters cut and gather the crops. Tankers carry the cows' milk from the farm to the city.

Busy wheels never stop! During the winter, snow-ploughs push the snow out of the road. Lorries dump cinders on the ice so tyres won't slip and slide. Special snow blowers make the snow fly into the air and out of the way. Wheels make the roads safe for other wheels.

Some people live on wheels. They drive their caravans and minibuses from place to place. Sometimes they stop just for the night. Sometimes they stay in the same place for a long time. Caravans have kitchens and beds and even bathrooms. A holiday home on wheels is fun.

Other people travel by aeroplane. Planes fly in the air, but on the ground they have to roll on wheels. The fuel trucks, the baggage trucks and the loading cranes also roll around the airfield.
Wheels are very busy at airports!

In the afternoon, wheels bring children home from school. Some children ride in school buses. Some ride on bicycles. Others travel by car.

After school, an ice-cream cone tastes good.
A van can bring ice cream right to your street.
Mail travels on wheels, too. And so do animals.
Wherever you look, something is rolling along.

At the end of the day, train wheels bring fathers and mothers back from the city. Car wheels are waiting to carry them home.

There are even wheels to carry wheels. Every day special railway cars take hundreds of new cars from the factory to all parts of the country. Then the cars are unloaded and travel for the first time on their own wheels.

Wheels have even gone to the moon, so the astronauts could travel around on moon dust.

Everywhere you look, busy wheels are turning!